FW

Plate 1
Fay Wray
King Kong (1933)

EL

Plate 2
Elsa Lanchester
Bride of Frankenstein (1935)

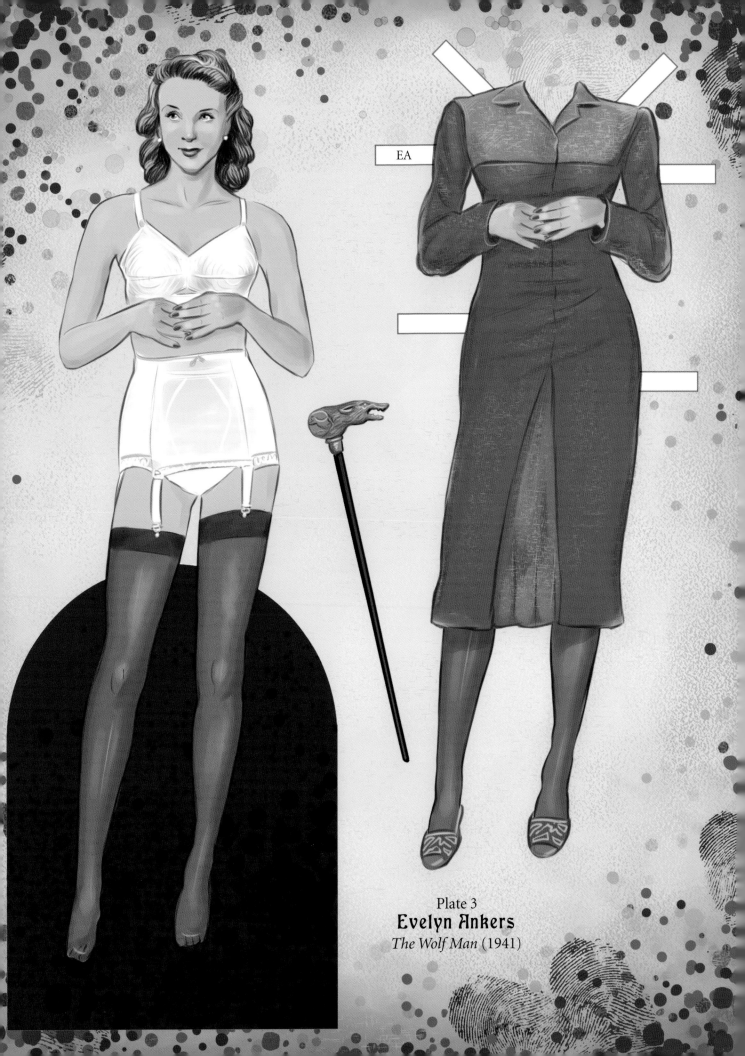

EA

Plate 3
Evelyn Ankers
The Wolf Man (1941)

JL

Plate 4
Janet Leigh
Psycho (1960)

BS

Plate 5
Barbara Steele
The Pit and the Pendulum
(1961)

TH

Plate 6
Tippi Hedren
The Birds (1963)

JO

Plate 7
Judith O'Dea
Night of the Living Dead
(1968)

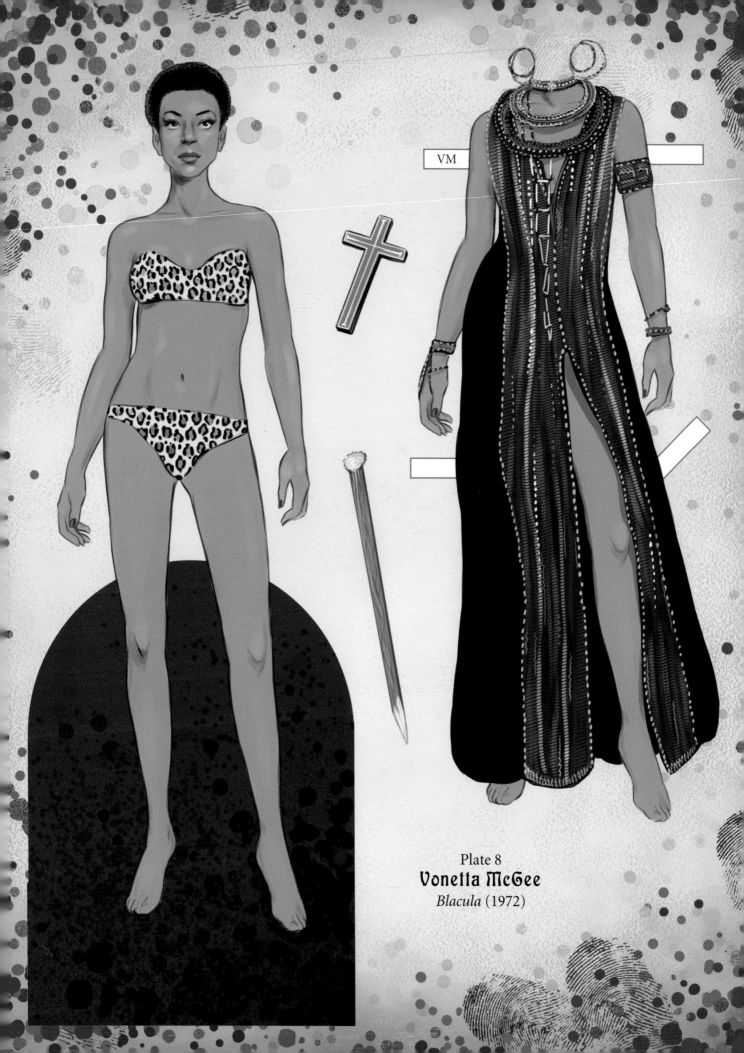

VM

Plate 8
Vonetta McGee
Blacula (1972)

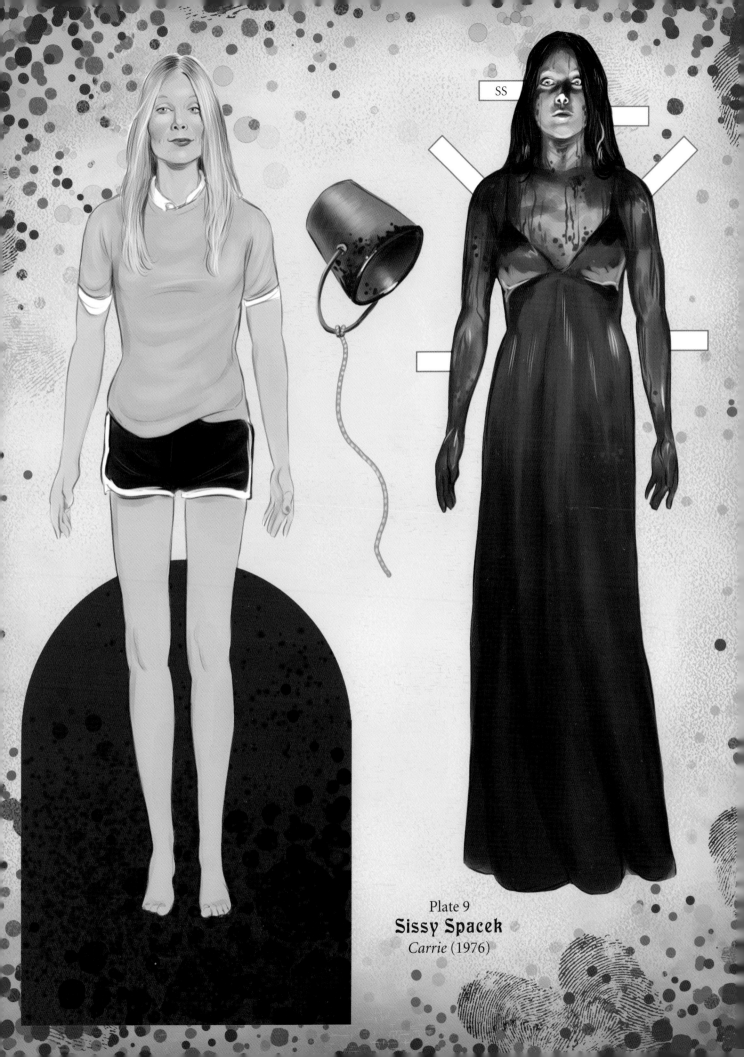

Plate 9
Sissy Spacek
Carrie (1976)

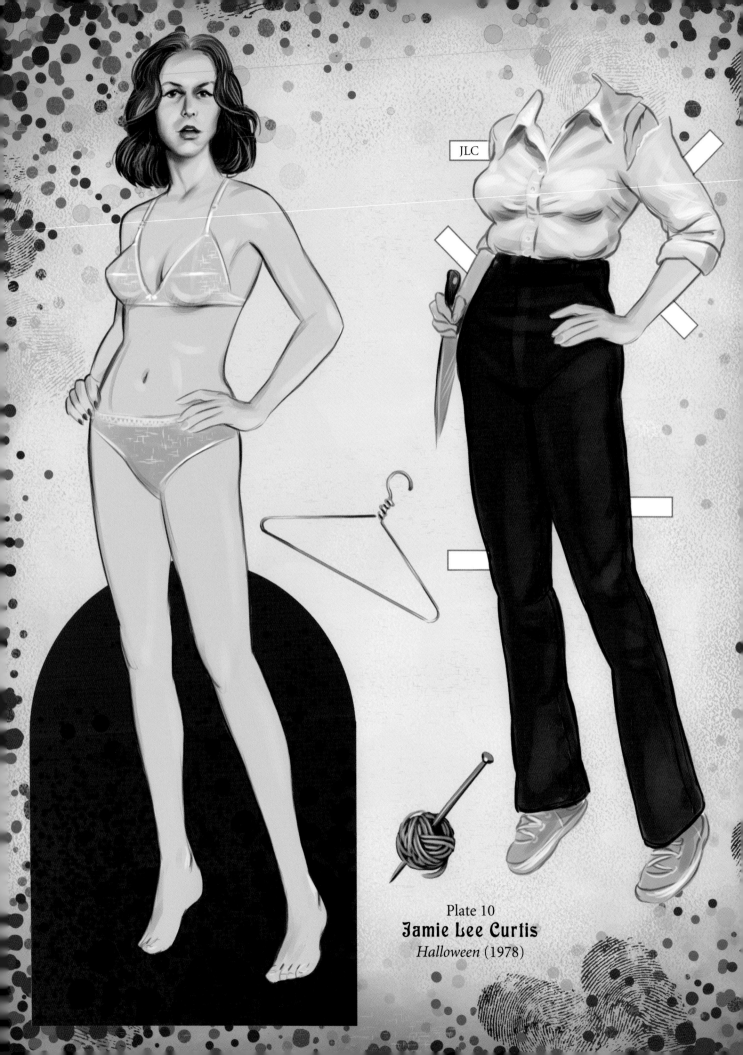

JLC

Plate 10
Jamie Lee Curtis
Halloween (1978)

HL

Plate 11
Heather Langenkamp
A Nightmare on Elm Street (1984)

NC

Plate 12
Neve Campbell
The Craft (1996)

SMG

Plate 13
Sarah Michelle Gellar
Buffy the Vampire Slayer
(1997–2003)

JT

Plate 14
Jennifer Tilly
Bride of Chucky (1998)

CM

Plate 15
Chloë Grace Moretz
Let Me In (2010)

Plate 16
Emma Roberts
*American Horror Story:
Coven (2013)*